HOW CAN A PIGEON Be a War Hero?

Tracey Turner lives in Bath and is the author of many non-fiction books for children, including *The Comic Strip History of the World* (and further Comic Strip titles), *101 Things You Need To Know . . . and Some You Don't!*, and the Hard Nuts of History series. This is her first title for Macmillan Children's Books.

Also in this series

Why Would a Dog Need a Parachute?
Jo Foster

TRACEY TURNER

HOW CAN A PIGEON Be a War Hero?

ILLUSTRATED BY ANDREW WIGHTMAN

In association with
Imperial War Museums

MACMILLAN CHILDREN'S BOOKS

First published 2014 by Macmillan Children's Books
a division of Macmillan Publishers Limited
20 New Wharf Road, London N1 9RR
Basingstoke and Oxford
Associated companies throughout the world
www.panmacmillan.com

In association with Imperial War Museums
IWM.org.uk

ISBN 978-1-4472-2619-2

3 5 7 9 8 6 4 2

A CIP catalogue record for this book is available from
the British Library.

Printed and bound by CPI Group (UK) Ltd, Croydon CR0 4YY

Thanks to Kira Andrews for her enthusiastic research for this book

The First World War 1914-1918

Why did the First World War start?

Had aeroplanes been invented yet?

Where did soldiers in the trenches go to the loo?

To find out, turn the page!

How did the First World War start?

Maybe you've heard answers to this question that start with an assassinated archduke, then Austria-Hungary and Imperial Germany and a Black Hand get involved, and after that things become more complicated and confusing until you end up wishing you'd never asked. It *is* a bit complicated. So take a deep breath, because we're about to become involved in empires, alliances and a struggle for world power.

By the beginning of the First World War, the powerful countries of Europe had been spoiling for a fight for some time, until one event started a chain reaction that led to war. But if that event hadn't happened, the strong likelihood is that something else would have started the war before very long anyway.

The main countries involved were . . .

Great Britain, which was nervous about Germany becoming too powerful and wanted to protect its trade routes, became friendly with France and Russia (even though it had a history of being their enemy). Britain also had an agreement that it would protect Belgium.

Great Britain

Belgium

France

France, which was big, powerful and suspicious of Germany, had formed an alliance with Russia in 1894.

Germany, which had become a country in 1871. Germany had a large army and an empire, and wanted to become even bigger and more powerful.

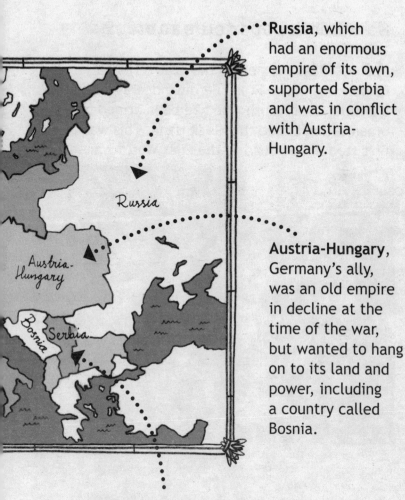

Russia, which had an enormous empire of its own, supported Serbia and was in conflict with Austria-Hungary.

Russia

Austria-Hungary

Bosnia   Serbia

Austria-Hungary, Germany's ally, was an old empire in decline at the time of the war, but wanted to hang on to its land and power, including a country called Bosnia.

Serbia, in south-eastern Europe, didn't want to become part of Austria-Hungary's empire and wanted to take control of Bosnia to form a greater Serbia.

So what happened *exactly*?

In June 1914, the heir to the Austro-Hungarian Empire, Archduke Franz Ferdinand, was killed by a Bosnian Serb youth who had been armed by an organisation called the Black Hand. This was the first step on the road to the First World War . . .

This photo of Franz Ferdinand of Austria and his wife was taken in Sarajevo in 1914, moments before they were assassinated.

- Austria-Hungary declared war on Serbia . . .
- Russia stuck up for Serbia, which caused Germany, Austria-Hungary's ally, to declare war on Russia . . .
- France, as Russia's ally, joined in and was now also at war with Germany and Austria-Hungary . . .

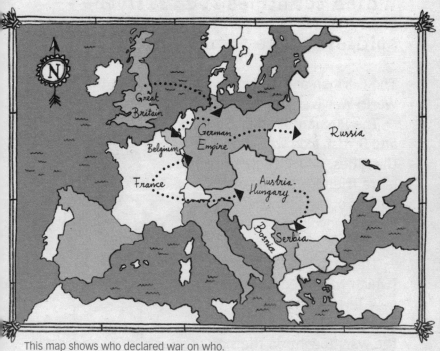

This map shows who declared war on who.

- Germany invaded the neutral country of Belgium, using it as the quickest route to attack the capital of France . . .
- Britain also entered the war, because it had promised to protect Belgium — but also because it wanted to stop Germany almost as much as France did.

These powerful countries, and others besides, were now involved in an absolutely massive fight — the biggest war there had ever been up to that point.

Which countries fought in the war (and where did all the soldiers come from)?

The German and Austro-Hungarian side in the First World War was known as the Central Powers.

The Russian, French, Serbian and British side was known as the Allies, which sounds much more friendly, but wasn't. Lots of other countries became involved on each side too:

The Ottoman Empire (which was ruled from what's now Turkey, and became the modern country of Turkey after the war) fought on the side of the Central Powers, and so did Bulgaria from October 1914. Italy also fought with the Allies from 1915 — even though they had been Germany and Austria-Hungary's ally before the war — and by 1916 so did Romania.

CENTRAL POWERS

Germans

Austro-Hungarians

Ottoman Empire

Bulgaria

ALLIES

Russian

French

Serbian

British

What about countries from outside of Europe?

Japan fought on the side of the Allies because it had an agreement with Britain. The United States fought against Germany and Austria-Hungary from 1917, but not against Turkey or Bulgaria.

Twenty-four different countries declared themselves at war with Germany or one of Germany's allies over the course of the war, though a lot of them didn't send any soldiers to fight. They included Panama (which didn't have an army at all), Costa Rica, Liberia, Haiti, Cuba, Brazil and Honduras.

A woman pins a flower to the tunic of an Indian soldier for luck.

As well as the countries that declared themselves at war, other countries around the world sent soldiers to fight. Great Britain had a vast empire (at its height, the British Empire was the biggest in the world, ever). It included Australia, Canada, India, New Zealand, the West Indies and the Union of South Africa, and soldiers from all of those countries fought alongside the Allies. More than 1.5 million soldiers from India fought in the war. Ireland was still part of Great Britain when the war broke out, and 210,000 Irish soldiers fought against the Central Powers in the war.

Why did Russia leave the War?

On top of fighting in the bloodiest war it had ever known, there was something else going on in Russia — something rather big, which became known as the Russian Revolution. This led to the country leaving the war in 1917.

What happened in the Russian Revolution?

There had been years of revolts against the Russian emperor, Tsar Nicholas, general strikes (when people refused to work if their demands weren't met), and demands for fairer conditions from ordinary people. The war against the Central Powers was unpopular because Russia had suffered serious defeats. Roughly 1.8 million Russians were killed in the war, with many more wounded or taken prisoner. In early 1917, the winter was especially hard, and there were food shortages. People who had been on strike began to riot, and were joined by government troops (who were supposed to be firing on the rioters, but joined in instead because they thought the rioters had a point).

Tsar Nicholas gave up his crown, and a government was formed by the revolutionaries. A few months later another revolution took place, led by a group called the Bolsheviks who took control of the capital city, Petrograd (now St Petersburg). One of the first things the Bolsheviks did was to get Russia out of the First World War. The fighting stopped, but the Bolsheviks had to give up vast chunks of land that belonged to the old Russian Empire. A Civil War began within Russia, which was eventually won by the Bolsheviks.

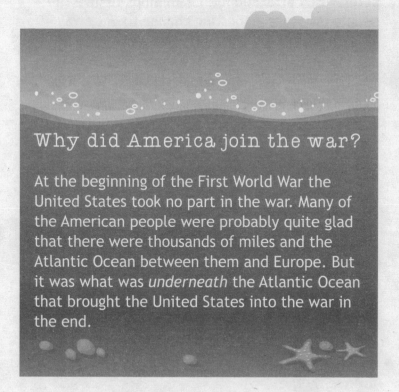

Why did America join the war?

At the beginning of the First World War the United States took no part in the war. Many of the American people were probably quite glad that there were thousands of miles and the Atlantic Ocean between them and Europe. But it was what was *underneath* the Atlantic Ocean that brought the United States into the war in the end.

What do you mean, *underneath* the Atlantic?

Lurking under the sea, German submarines known as U-boats launched torpedoes at shipping. The ships might be enemy battleships, or they might be transporting goods and passengers (merchant ships), even if they were from countries that weren't at war. At first, U-boats used to surface before they attacked merchant ships to give the people on board a sporting chance to get away in lifeboats before their ship was blown up. This put the attacking U-boat in danger, and from 1915 onwards Germany decided not to be quite so sporting, and sunk ships without giving them a warning first. Passenger liners with American

citizens aboard were sunk, and the United States looked as though it might be angry enough to join the war, so Germany stopped surprise attacks on shipping for almost a year and a half. But it went back to surprise attacks on merchant ships from February 1917, because it was such an effective way of battering the Allies. The U-boats were very successful: in the next two months, they sank more than 500 merchant ships. By April 1917, the United States had had enough of the loss of their ships, and entered the war.

There was another reason the United States joined the war: a secret coded message from Germany to Mexico had been intercepted and decoded. The message asked Mexico to join the war on the side of the Central Powers, in return for big bits of the United States once the war was over. The British decoded it and made sure the US president saw it.

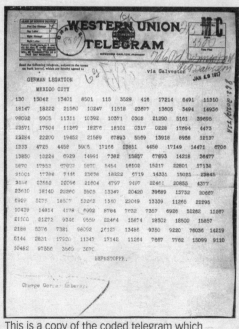

This is a copy of the coded telegram which was sent in 1917.

How many people fought in the war?

The First World War really was a *world* war — from the European countries where it began, the war spread to Africa, Asia and the Middle East, and soldiers came from even further afield — the United States, the West Indies, Australia and New Zealand. So it's no surprise that lots of people were involved, but even so the number of soldiers is staggering. Altogether, over 65 million people fought in the war — more than the entire population of the United Kingdom today. Almost nine million men from the British Empire fought in the war.

Each soldier represents one million soldiers:

British soldiers

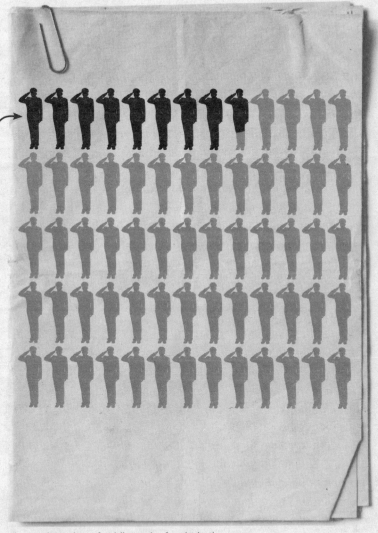

The total number of soldiers who fought in the war.

Did women fight in the war?

Women did fight in the Russian army, but not in any of the others (with a couple of exceptions). At first, Russian women weren't allowed to fight, but some did anyway — either they disguised themselves as men, or they used their influence to get around the rules. In 1917, women's units were formed in the Russian army, including the terrifyingly named Battalion of Death. Altogether about 6,000 women fought in the Russian army.

Members of the Russian women's 'Battalion of Death' training in Petrograd.

In Britain and the other countries in the war, women didn't fight but got involved in the war in other ways. British women of the Women's Army Auxiliary Corps worked as army drivers, cooks, and in mechanical, technical and office jobs at home and abroad — more than 57,000 women served in it, and there were similar women's services set up for the navy and the air force. Women also worked at home in other ways in support of the war (see page 110).

Female soldiers in Russia's army had their heads completely shaved.

So there weren't *any* British female solders?

Flora Sandes was an exception to the rule: she was one of only two British women to serve as a soldier in the First World War. She joined the St John's Ambulance service as a nurse and went to Serbia, where she enrolled in the Serbian army. She was badly wounded in hand-to-hand fighting in 1916, and received a medal for bravery and a promotion to Sergeant Major (and after the war she was promoted to Captain). A few other Serbian women fought in Serbia's army, too.

The only other *known* British woman to serve as a soldier was called Dorothy Lawrence. Using disguises and fake papers, she managed to make her way to the Somme posing as a male British soldier, and was set to work as a 'sapper' or military engineer, laying mines under fire only 400 metres from the front line. After ten days of

service she presented herself to the commanding officer, who had her immediately placed under military arrest and

Sergeant Major Flora Sandes during her rehabilitation from wounds inflicted during the war.

then interrogated as a spy.

The army were embarrassed that a woman had managed to breach their security and also worried that if her story got out, more women would want to join the army or take on men's jobs. Eventually Dorothy was sent back to London, however she was forbidden from publishing anything about her experience, and her story was not discovered until many years after her death.

Did any children fight?

Children weren't supposed to fight — the minimum age for soldiers was 18 in Britain — but lots of patriotic boys lied about their age and joined the army anyway. Many of them were discovered and sent back home, but lots of them weren't and did fight in the war. The first British soldier to be killed on the Western Front died in August 1914 — he was called John Parr, and he was just seventeen years old.

Several boys were younger still: a newspaper story from 1916 mentions a Private S. Lewis who served in France, who was only twelve when he joined the army. Tens of thousands of underage soldiers fought in the war.

Were people forced to fight?

Some countries that fought in the war, such as Germany, France and Russia, had large armies even when they weren't at war because they 'conscripted' men of a certain age to be soldiers for a number of years. The British army was very small in comparison because Britain didn't have conscription — the army was made up of soldiers who had chosen the army as their profession.

Once the war started, Britain needed more men to fight. Lord Kitchener, the Secretary of State for War, starred in a recruitment poster which featured a portrait of Kitchener looking very serious and pointing at the viewer, with the words 'Britons, Kitchener wants you!' Kitchener's direct approach worked: thanks to his recruitment drive, thousands of British men volunteered for service, as well as men from different parts of the British Empire.

If you volunteered for the army, could you stay with your mates?

Yes, sometimes you could. 'Pals' battalions were groups of friends or colleagues who fought together in the same fighting unit — the first one was made up of stockbrokers from the City of London who all volunteered together. This meant that the men could fight alongside people they knew well and liked, but it could also mean that a whole community's young men could suffer terrible loss if the battalion came under heavy fire. Thousands of men from all over Britain, but especially the north, volunteered to fight in pals battalions in 1914 and 1915.

A group of 'Leeds Pals' at their training camp in the Yorkshire Dales shortly after enlisting, 1914.

IT IS FAR BETTER
TO FACE THE BULLETS
THAN TO BE KILLED
AT HOME BY A BOMB

JOIN THE ARMY AT ONCE
& HELP TO STOP AN AIR RAID

GOD SAVE THE KING

In 1916, Britain introduced conscription: all fit single men aged between 18 and 41 had to join the army or the navy, unless they were single because their wife had died and they had children to look after, or unless they were a church minister. Men who did certain jobs important to the government or to the war were excluded. Married men had to join up after June 1916, and eventually the age limit was raised to 51.

In Britain, men had the right to refuse to fight in the war. Some men refused because they were pacifists (they thought all wars were wrong) or because they didn't believe that particular war was right. These men were known as 'conscientious objectors', and most had to work in jobs that helped the war effort, but without actually fighting. Men who refused were sent to prison.

Why were some men given white feathers?

At the beginning of the war, Admiral Charles Fitzgerald founded the Order of the White Feather in order to shame young men into joining the army, if they hadn't already. The idea was that people should give white feathers to men who weren't in one of the armed forces, as a symbol of cowardice.

Some people were very enthusiastic in their handing out of white feathers: they were given to men who weren't fit to fight, or were too young but looked older, or even to soldiers home on leave and not dressed in uniform. Men who worked for the government in the war effort, and so wore ordinary clothes, were given special badges to explain their lack of uniform.

Posh older men had a special code

of conduct when accusing men of cowardice: rather than just handing out white feathers, they thought it was more polite to give out calling cards (which had their name and address printed on them) with the feathers, so that the man receiving the feather would know who sent it, and had a chance to send a reply.

Who was in charge of the armies?

In overall charge of the armies were the people who ran the countries involved — all of them men, because at the time in most countries women weren't even allowed to vote in elections, let alone run countries. Commanders of the armies reported to them.

So governments and monarchs were in charge, not army commanders?

That's right. The Prime Minister of Great Britain when the war started was Herbert Asquith, and David Lloyd George became Prime Minister in 1916. Field Marshal John French was in charge of the British forces on the Western Front, until he

Herbert Asquith.

was replaced in 1915 by Douglas Haig.

Germany didn't have an elected leader — instead, the monarch, Kaiser Wilhelm II, was in charge of the country. He was Queen Victoria's grandson (she'd died in 1901), and so were English King George V and Tsar Nicholas, who was in charge of

David Lloyd George.

Russia (until 1917 and the Russian Revolution). It was a big, unhappy family, Queen Victoria's grandchildren at war with each other. The German army's Commander-in-chief was Paul von Hindenburg.

This poster of Paul von Hindenburg from 1917 was used to encourage German people to support the war.

The French President was Raymond Poincaré, with Georges Clemenceau as minister for war and Prime Minister from 1917. Joseph Joffre was Commander-in-chief of the French until after the Battle of Verdun in 1916, when he was replaced by Robert Nivelle. After French army mutinies in 1917, Nivelle was replaced by Philippe Pétain.

A French commander-in-chief of all the Allied armies, Ferdinand Foch, was appointed in the spring of 1918.

A Big Unhappy Family Tree

Queen Victoria was King George'

Queen Victori

Queen Victoria

English

Kaiser Wilhelm II

German

Queen Victoria was Kaiser Wilhelm's grandmother

King George V's grandmother

Kaiser Wilhelm II and King George V were cousins

King George V and Tsar Nicholas were cousins

King George V

English

was Tsar Nicholas's grandmother

Tsar Nicholas

Russian

Kaiser Wilhelm II and Tsar Nicholas were cousins

Because so many soldiers were killed and injured early on in the war, none of the countries' leaders felt that they could end the war other than by winning it. To keep it going, the countries had to churn out massive numbers of guns and ammunition, and borrow money to pay for them.

What were the different uniforms like?

Today, most people think that camouflage seems like the obvious way to dress a soldier — after all, soldiers don't want to advertise their positions and risk getting shot. But in the nineteenth century, armies dressed in bright regimental colours, announcing where they were to the opposing army and so that there could be no doubt about who was who. By the First World War, things were very different.

British soldiers' uniforms were khaki, a green-brown wool mix, and the other armies mostly went for muted grey-ish colours, apart from the French, who wore a grey blue. At the beginning of the war, German soldiers had spiked

A German soldier in uniform.

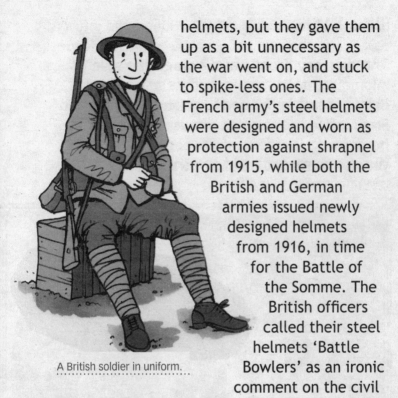

helmets, but they gave them up as a bit unnecessary as the war went on, and stuck to spike-less ones. The French army's steel helmets were designed and worn as protection against shrapnel from 1915, while both the British and German armies issued newly designed helmets from 1916, in time for the Battle of the Somme. The British officers called their steel helmets 'Battle Bowlers' as an ironic comment on the civil servants and politicians who they saw as interfering with the running of the war at the Front.

A British soldier in uniform.

Where did the fighting happen?

Battle zones, where wars are actually fought, are known as 'fronts'. Most of the big battles of the First World War were fought on the Western Front, which was the line that marked the edge of the German attacking army (it was the furthest west they'd managed to invade).

The Different Fronts

The Western Front was a battle zone several kilometres deep, and snaked its way from the Belgian coast in the north, through Belgium and France down to the Alps mountain range at the border with Switzerland. Its position changed as the war continued and territory was won and lost.

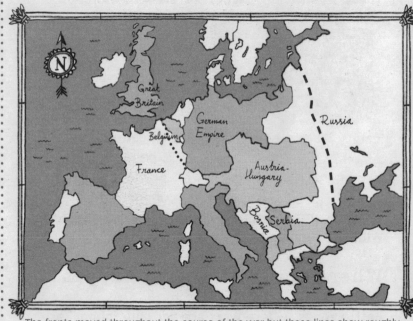

The fronts moved throughout the course of the war but these lines show roughly where they were.

•••••••••••••• Western Front

– – – – – – – Eastern Front

There was fighting in many other parts of the world too. Germany and Austria-Hungary fought Russia on **the Eastern Front**, which stretched from Riga (which is now the capital of Latvia) in the north down to Czernowitz in what's now Ukraine in the south. Fighting on the Eastern Front continued until 1917, when Russia left the war to concentrate on having a revolution. In Serbia, fierce fighting raged as Austria-Hungary and then the combined Central Powers invaded the country, until Serbia was defeated in 1915.

Further away, the Allies fought the Ottoman Empire in various parts of the Middle East. In Africa there was fighting between British Empire troops and German troops, because different African countries were part of the British and German Empires. Even China and some Pacific islands became involved in the war, as the Allies captured land there that belonged to Germany. Furthest away of all, the waters around the British Falkland Islands in the South Atlantic were the scene of a sea battle in 1914 — the islands are about 500 km from the coast of Argentina, and 13,000 km from Britain.

What was the Arab Revolt?

The Ottoman Empire had ruled the Middle East for 400 years, but by the beginning of the twentieth century it was weak. Sherif Hussen bin Ali wanted to unite the Arab people for the first time and end Turkish rule. In 1916, Arab forces successfully attacked the Turks, but the Turkish army sent more troops and weapons to stop them. The Arabs needed modern weapons and supplies.

It suited the British to have the Turkish army fighting the Arabs in the Middle East instead of fighting them, or other Allies, somewhere else. After the Ottoman victory at Gallipoli (see page 40), the British were especially worried that the Ottomans would attack British military bases in Egypt, and were keen to protect the rich oil fields of the Middle East, and the Suez Canal, which

T. E. Lawrence in traditional Arabian dress.

provided them with a valuable trade route. Britain encouraged the Arab uprising and gave the Arabs weapons. T. E. Lawrence was one of the British officers sent to help the Arabs. He became known as Lawrence of Arabia, and led the Arabs in a guerrilla war in the desert. With the Ottoman army busy, the British took control of Jerusalem, and the Arab and British armies joined forces against the Ottoman Empire.

What happened to the ordinary people who lived near the Western Front?

It was very bad luck for the people who lived there that one of the bloodiest wars in history was fought in northern France and Belgium. As the Germans advanced, they occupied towns and villages and the people there had to stay put and do as they were told by the invaders.

As the Allied soldiers moved forward to meet the invading Germany army, people living in the war zone had to move out, and either went to stay with relatives somewhere else, or became refugees. Allied soldiers watched sad columns of people fleeing the fighting trudging away with their possessions in

bundles, some leading or riding farm animals.

In farmhouses and villages close to the Front, life went on as normal (or as close to normal as possible), with farmers ploughing their fields and children playing within a couple of kilometres of the fighting. If they were close enough, buildings suffered damage from shells, and sometimes civilians were killed. Soldiers sometimes shared farmhouses with farming families, farmworkers and animals — they often had to sleep in haylofts or animal stalls. Towns and villages near the front line but out of the range of the guns provided a rest for soldiers when they weren't at the Front.

Many of the towns and villages of the Western Front were so battered by the fighting that they ended up in ruins. Some were completely flattened and never rebuilt.

What happened at Gallipoli?

The Gallipoli peninsula is a finger of land that points into the Mediterranean Sea. On one side of it, the Dardanelles is a narrow, 60-mile-long stretch of water that links the Mediterranean and the Sea of Marmara, dividing Europe from Asia. It's an important trade route — most of Russia's grain used to be brought through it — but the Ottoman Empire had closed it to the Allies.

Gallipoli peninsula

Bulgaria

Turkey

Greece

At the end of 1914 the entrenched armies on the Western Front weren't making much progress one way or the other. The British and French decided to attack the Dardanelles, and then the plan was to attack the capital of the Ottoman Empire, Constantinople (now Istanbul), in the hope of defeating the Ottomans and weakening the Central Powers, and restoring Russia's trade route.

In February 1915 British and French ships attacked Turkish forts in the Dardanelles, but lots of them were sunk by Turkish mines. Even though the Allies had been defeated at sea, two months later French and British troops, and a large number

A group of Turkish officers. Dardanelles, 1915.

of Australian and New Zealand soldiers, landed on the Gallipoli peninsula and attacked the Turkish army.

The Turkish army wasn't as weak as the French and British had predicted. They fought on for months, in trenches like the ones on the Western Front (see page 44) — except a lot hotter during the Mediterranean summer. Food spoiled quickly and disease spread. Altogether, more than half a million soldiers died or were wounded at Gallipoli, with heavy losses on both sides. Eventually, at the end of 1915 and the beginning of the following year, Allied troops were evacuated. The Ottoman army had won the battle, and the aims of the Allies ended in failure and a massive loss of life.

Were there any sea battles?

As well as the attack on the Dardanelles (see above), sea battles took place in the Falklands (see page 35), the Mediterranean and the North Sea.

The biggest sea battle was the Battle of Jutland in the North Sea, involving 250 British and German ships. German Admiral Scheer planned to attack the British battle cruisers commanded by Admiral Beatty, then attack the main British fleet, commanded by Admiral Jellicoe, once he'd dealt with the first lot. British code breakers managed to warn the navy of Scheer's plans, so the British fleets were prepared. In the end, both sides lost ships and men and the British side lost the most: 14 ships and 6,094 men, while the Germans lost 11 ships and 2,551 men. Even so, it was enough to convince the Germans who had fewer ships in their navy than the British, not to attack in the North Sea again.

The naval blockade of the North Sea was another way of waging war. The huge and powerful British navy stopped enemy ships from entering the North Sea and the English Channel, to stop supplies headed for Germany and Austria-Hungary. Ships from neutral countries were allowed, but if they were carrying cargo bound for Germany or Austria-Hungary, the British took the cargo. The Central

The total number of German and British ships

German ships lost

British ships lost

Powers found substitutes for the materials they needed to make weapons and supplies for the army, but the blockade on food, added to bad harvests, meant that people went hungry and in some cases starved.

German submarine attacks were partly a response to the naval blockade, and increased after the Battle of Jutland. The United States joined the war partly as a result of these attacks (see page 14).

What were the trenches?

Massive great guns capable of firing long distances were used in the First World War. Their devastating fire power drove each side to shelter in trenches. At first, these were just shallow ditches to provide cover, but before long they'd become complex systems of deep trenches where soldiers could keep a permanent base. The trenches were fortified with machine-gun positions and newly invented barbed wire to stop surprise attacks. The lines of trenches were arranged in zigzags, so that if a shell dropped on one part of the trench, damage would be limited. Trenches had been used in warfare before 1914, but not to such an extent or for such a long time. The invading Germans wanted to hang on to the ground they'd gained, the Allied forces tried to push them back. Big guns blazed from one side to the other as each side tried to come up with new tactics or technology that would break the stalemate.

British trenches in the Somme.

Every so often a battle would take place, as one side tried to gain ground, often with huge numbers of soldiers killed and wounded.

The Germans' plan was to dig in and hold on to the ground they'd already captured. They had the best positions on higher ground, which gave them an advantage over the Allies, who had to attack them uphill. Because the German trenches were intended to be more permanent than the British and French ones, they were much more solid and better equipped. The Germans lined them with cement, made them two or three storeys deep in some places, and some had electric lights, water tanks with taps, and even doorbells and wallpaper.

What was it like living in the trenches?

Some parts of the trenches were bombarded with artillery almost all the time, while in others things were much quieter. Today, people often think of the trenches as freezing cold, barren and full of water — and sometimes they were. But the temperature could be very warm in summertime, and the soldiers often had to cut back the undergrowth in spring and summer so that they could see the enemy positions.

Different parts of the trenches saw different conditions: the thick clay of Belgium meant especially muddy conditions, while the area around the River Somme in France was chalky. In some places the ground was too wet to dig down, so the soldiers built mounds of earth to make above-ground trenches called 'breastworks'.

What was no-man's-land?

No-man's-land was the strip of ground that separated the two lines of trenches on the Western Front, on one side the Germans, on the other the Allies. It was usually between about 100 and 300 metres wide. Especially at night, soldiers set out into no-man's-land in order to find out about the other side's position and defences, and to carry out raids. Raids on opposing trenches first involved cutting through the barbed wire that protected the trenches, crawling through, then using weapons such as knives and hand grenades to attack the enemy trench.

Did soldiers really play football in no-man's-land at Christmas?

Lots of people had predicted the war would be over by Christmas, so the soldiers in the trenches on the Western Front on Christmas Day 1914 were disappointed that they weren't tucking into Christmas dinner with their families instead. On one part of the front line on Christmas Eve, British soldiers heard the Germans singing carols and began to shout messages across to them. On Christmas Day, British and German soldiers met in no-man's-land and swapped presents and took photos. Some had a kick about — we don't know the score, but the Germans won. The truce was also an opportunity for both sides to gather the dead bodies in no-man's-land and take them away for burial, and to make repairs on the trenches. After Boxing Day, there were no more carols or Christmas greetings — the soldiers went

This photo is of British and German soldiers spending time together on Christmas Day, 1914.

back to business which, unfortunately, meant killing one another.

There were a few places along the front line where soldiers called a ceasefire and got together with their enemies in the opposing trenches over Christmas 1914. But it didn't happen everywhere along the Western Front, and in some places there were attacks, with soldiers wounded and killed over the Christmas period. Some of the French soldiers who'd made friends with the Germans that Christmas were court-martialled — tried in a military court — because of it. After that first Christmas of the war, there were no more Christmas truces.

What did soldiers do when they weren't fighting?

Soldiers didn't spend all their time on the front line. Away from it they trained, kept equipment and weapons clean and tidy, and looked after the animals that played their part in the war (see page 65). In their free time, one of the things soldiers looked forward to most was reading letters from friends and family at home, and they also spent lots of time writing replies. When it was their turn for a well-earned rest, they might go to a bar for a meal and a drink, and have a good night's sleep.

Sometimes more artistic soldiers made things from bits and pieces they found lying around — they might make jewellery from scraps of metal, or sew tapestries. These creations are known as 'trench art', though they weren't usually made inside the trenches themselves.

French, British and American soldiers enjoy leave on the beach at Boulogne, France, in 1918.

Were there toilets in the trenches?

There were no flushing loos in the trenches, but then again plenty of houses in Britain didn't have flushing loos either — they had outhouses outside, which were sheds enclosing a pit with a seat on it, and might be shared with several neighbouring houses.

DO NOT ENTER! LATRINES OVERFLOWING

In the trenches, a top priority was for good deep toilet pits to be dug. It was a priority because if human poo is left lying around, it isn't just horrible: fatal diseases can spread. And where lots of people live close together, disease can spread very quickly. The toilet pits in the trenches usually had wooden toilet seats on top. When a pit was full it had to be covered over — and a big sign put up to tell everyone of the horrors underneath — and another pit dug.

Did the officers in charge have to use the toilet pits too?

Not necessarily. There were separate latrines for officers, which were probably a bit less smelly because they weren't used by as many people. How long the latrine trench had been there made a difference to how horrible it was, too. The Germans, with their superior trenches, had better toilets too.

These freezing cold latrines in Leaevillers, France, show you just what toilet conditions could be like on the Western Front.

53

What did soldiers eat?

British soldiers were given a ration of food every day that aimed to give them 4,193 calories. That sounds like a lot — adult men today are supposed to have around 2,500, but then again they spend a lot of time lounging about watching telly. The number of calories for the soldiers of the First World War was worked out to be the amount a fit, active young man needed when doing hard physical work in the cold.

Women in a factory pack up grocery rations for soldiers.

Soldiers often found the food a bit boring, but at least there was enough of it — most of the time, anyway — and for some of the soldiers it might even be an improvement on what they ate at home: not everyone in those days had enough to eat, and discoveries about the importance of vitamins and a balanced diet were only just starting to be made. The soldiers were given:

- Fresh or frozen meat, plus bully beef (preserved meat) and bacon — they'd get quite a lot of meat every day
- Bread
- Cheese
- Some rice and oatmeal
- Condensed milk
- Tea
- Jam and sugar

That doesn't sound very healthy! What about vegetables?

Even though it doesn't sound as though they were getting their five-a-day, British soldiers were better off than French and German soldiers. French soldiers complained bitterly about the poor quality of their rations (which contained half a litre of wine a day!). German soldiers' rations were very often not enough, partly because of the blockade by Allied ships that stopped supplies reaching Germany, and led to widespread hunger in the country as the war went on.

On Christmas Day, a special effort was made to make a Christmas dinner, but sometimes things didn't go to plan. In December 1915, two geese were bought to be fattened up for Christmas, but the British soldiers grew so fond of the birds that they named them Jimmy and Jane and made them army mascots instead. Jimmy and Jane both survived until long after the war was over.

Jimmy

Jane

Could soldiers keep in touch with their families?

They may not have had email, Skype or instant messaging, but soldiers could keep in touch with their families more efficiently than you might think. Sending post was much quicker in those days than it is now, and it became even more efficient when post codes were introduced during the war to speed up the mail. Soldiers on the Western Front could expect to receive letters from home the day after they were written. It wasn't instant — but at least keeping in touch was like having a conversation, rather than out-of-date news bulletins every so often.

How did soldiers communicate with one another when they were far apart?

By the time of the First World War, telephone technology had been around for a while (though it was very rare for people to have telephones in their homes), and telephones were used in the trenches.

But phones in those days relied on wires, which could be easily damaged. So if soldiers needed to communicate, they could send a runner (a person who ran as fast as possible, maybe dodging enemy fire), or a rider on horseback or sometimes on bikes or motorbikes. Dogs and pigeons were also used as messengers (see pages 65 and 68). Semaphore — a coded system of sending messages with flags — was also used, as

long as the sender and receiver of the semaphore message were well out of the enemy's sight.
Radio had been invented and didn't rely on wires, but it was easy for the enemy to intercept the messages.

Did soldiers get holidays?

Soldiers did get holidays, but they didn't very often get to go home to their families, and sometimes they stayed away from home for months. Officers were more likely to get home leave than ordinary soldiers. But soldiers did get lots of leave away from battle — the average was about four days in any two-week period actually fighting on the front line. This meant that some soldiers were able to visit places they never would have had the chance to see otherwise.

Four British sergeants pose with their camels on a trip to the pyramids and the Sphinx in Egypt.

Who were the war artists and war poets?

From 1916, a group of British artists was sponsored by the government to paint eyewitness scenes of the war. Their paintings included battles and trenches, landscapes torn apart by bomb craters, wounded soldiers, the first tanks, battleships at sea, and munitions factories at home. The images were used to influence people's attitudes towards the war. One of the aims of the Imperial

A picture by Adrian Hill, who was an artist commissioned to paint life in the trenches.

This painting by William Orpen shows the shelled streets of Combles, France.

War Museum, which was founded in 1917, was to collect images of the First World War, and the museum commissioned artists too. Some of the best known war artists are John Singer Sargent, Paul Nash, Augustus John and William Orpen.

61

War poets weren't commissioned by the government as the war artists were, they were just people who were involved in the war and wrote poems about it. Some of them had had their poems published before the war, others only had their work published afterwards. The poems express personal experiences of the war and the poets' feelings about it. Some of them have become famous, and people still read them today — they've been gathered together in anthologies,

Siegfried Sassoon.

and you might study them at school. Some of the most famous war poets are Rupert Brooke and Wilfred Owen, who both died in the war, and Siegfried Sassoon, who survived it. Sassoon gained a reputation for bravery and earned the nickname Mad Jack, but his anti-war beliefs, reflected in his poetry, upset some people at the time he was writing.

Why were horses used in the war?

A hundred years ago there were no motorways, and very few people owned cars. Horses and oxen still pulled carts and ploughs on farms, and carried passengers in horse-drawn vehicles. Petrol-engined cars had been invented in the 1880s, and cars, lorries and motorbikes (and later tanks) were used in the war, but horses were still the best and fastest way to travel across country. They were used to haul wagons and guns about, carry messengers, and to attack the enemy in cavalry charges (soldiers mounted on horses galloping towards the enemy).

Before the First World War, cavalry attacks were an important battle tactic. At the beginning of the war, in August 1914, one of the first battles was led by cavalry. After the soldiers had dug trenches

63

on the Western Front, it was still thought that the cavalry would be used. The idea was that once the big guns and soldiers had made a break in the enemy line, right back to the last line of defences, the cavalry would gallop through into enemy territory, leading to a glorious victory. Hurray! But real breaks in the enemy line rarely ever happened — the trenches were much easier to defend than they were to attack. Modern weapons and trench warfare made the cavalry out of date. Horses were no match against newly invented machine guns, heavy artillery and barbed wire. Finally, they were replaced by tanks, which were invented during the First World War.

A horse-drawn ambulance at the Battle of Ypres, 1914.

What other animals were involved in the war?

As well as horses, the army used mules (a cross between a horse and a donkey) for moving things around. They also used messenger dogs — dogs that had been trained to talk and deliver messages. Not really. The dogs were trained to run from one place to another carrying a message in a metal tube attached to their collars — the prospect of food at the other end encouraged them to go where they were supposed to, though some dogs proved more reliable than others.

Soldiers often rescued pets that were lost or abandoned after their owners had to leave because of the war — cats, parrots, canaries, rabbits and dogs. One stray dog had been wounded and had a missing paw — soldiers named the dog Thelus after the village where he was found, healed the wound and made the dog an artificial leg, after which he ran about quite happily.

Winnie the bear.

Fighting units often had 'mascots' — special pets that belonged to the unit. Many of them were dogs, and there were lots of goats and horses, but there were some more unusual animals too: Jackie the baboon was the mascot of the 3rd South African Infantry (Transvaal Regiment) — he spent three years on the Western Front and survived the war, though he lost a leg; Nancy the springbok was another South African mascot; and Winnipeg the black bear was the mascot of a Canadian cavalry regiment — though Winnie was kept away from the fighting. She was left at London Zoo before her regiment travelled to France, where she became the inspiration for A. A. Milne's *Winnie the Pooh*.

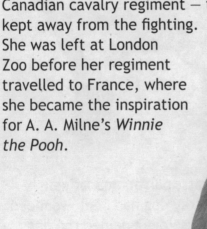

Did soldiers like having animals around?

Not always. Often, soldiers often grew fond of animals, which helped cheer them up, just like our pets do if we're having a bad day. But not all animals were welcome. Rats thrived in the trenches, living on waste food and unburied dead people and animals, and dogs that were good 'ratters' were prized. Soldiers didn't get a chance to wash themselves or their clothes very regularly, and were plagued with lice, which made homes in their clothing and lived on their blood, making the men itch unbearably. Soldiers spent a lot of time looking through the seams of their clothes to discover the lice, which they squashed with a cracking sound or burned with a candle. Hours were spent hunting for the hated parasites, and the soldiers never seemed to be able to get rid of them completely.

67

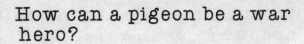

How can a pigeon be a war hero?

Pigeons were also used as messengers during the war. Homing pigeons can find their way back to their loft, and several thousand of the birds were available to carry messages clipped in metal containers to their legs. Pigeons were more reliable than dogs, and less easy a target for the enemy to shoot — though they were often shot, and both sides also used hawks to stop the enemy's pigeons from delivering their messages. Bad weather made it difficult for pigeons to deliver messages, too. One pigeon in particular became famous. Cher Ami (which is French for 'dear friend') was a carrier pigeon flown by the US Army Signal Corps in France. The pigeon delivered twelve messages at the Battle of the Argonne.

What happened to Cher Ami at the Battle of the Argonne?

On her last mission, the tough old pigeon was shot through the breast by enemy fire but still managed to return to her loft, where her message was retrieved from the remains of her badly damaged leg. The message was from a battalion that had been isolated from the rest of the American forces — the two previous pigeons they'd sent with messages asking for help had been shot down, and Cher Ami was their last hope. The message enabled 194 of the men to be rescued. Cher Ami was posthumously awarded the French medal for heroism in battle, the Croix de Guerre with Palm. The pigeon wasn't really brave — she was just doing what homing pigeons do — but it's true that without homing pigeons delivering messages, more men might have died, and it's true that Cher Ami's message saved the isolated soldiers. Stories like Cher Ami's helped to cheer everyone up, too.

The Croix de Guerre.

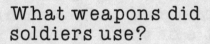

What weapons did soldiers use?

The Industrial Revolution, which changed manufacture from small-scale cottage industry at the end of the eighteenth century to mass-producing factories in the nineteenth century, had changed life completely, and it changed war too. Weapons and ammunition were made in factories in their millions, and were more powerful than ever before.

In 1914, the destruction that newly invented weapons of war could cause came as a shock to both sides. Huge great artillery guns, which could be quickly reloaded and didn't need to be aimed between shots, fired enormous shells that gouged deep craters into the landscape.

That sounds scary. How big were the shells?

The biggest shells fired on the Western Front were about 38 cm in diameter, which is wider than this open book. The shells could travel further and cause more damage than ever before, and everyone was horrified at the numbers of dead and wounded. By the end of 1914, not even six months into the war, a million men had been killed on both sides, with another four million wounded. The trenches were dug as a result.

These big guns were responsible for seven out of every ten casualties throughout the war. Hundreds of millions of shells were fired on the Western Front — some of them failed to explode, and the buried unexploded shells still blow up and kill people on First World War battlefields in Belgium and France today.

Deep underground, soldiers dug tunnels reaching under enemy territory and planted mines, which could be set off with an electrical signal. The mines were sometimes enormous: the biggest was exploded at Spanbroekmolen at the start of the Battle of Messines in 1917. It contained more than 40,000 kg of explosive and caused a crater 27 metres across and 12 metres deep, which filled with water because of the clay soil and high water table in the area. It's still there today, and is known as the 'Pool of Peace'. The sound of the explosion was clearly heard in London, about 250 km away.

Trench mortars were large but portable guns for firing shells. They could be set up in trenches and

used as an instant response to fire from opposing trenches (whereas the big guns way behind the front line wouldn't know where to fire straight away).

Stacks of shells at a factory in Chilwell, Nottinghamshire.

What other weapons did soldiers in the trenches use?

Soldiers in the trenches used smaller guns, which had become more effective too — machine guns could fire more bullets faster than ever before, up to 600 bullets per minute — and there was a machine gun for every platoon of 50 or so men. Each individual soldier was also armed with a rifle and a bayonet (a long knife attached to the end of the rifle).

Two British soldiers wearing gas masks man a machine gun at the Battle of the Somme.

Vast quantities of weapons were produced: 4 million rifles, 250,000 machine guns, 52,000 planes, 25,000 big artillery guns and 170 million rounds of shells were produced in Britain alone during the First World War.

Why did soldiers still fight with swords?

At first, British officers still carried swords, as they had in previous wars — which might seem like a strange thing to do, but the big guns of the First World War were new technology. Officers stopped carrying swords about a year into the war. Apart from the fact that they weren't much use against guns, the swords helped enemy soldiers identify the officers, who were more important targets because they were in charge. All soldiers had knives to use in case of hand-to-hand fighting.

British cavalry soldiers were armed with a sword and a lance — a long stick with a blade attached to the end — until 1915 when they stopped using the sword, but kept the lance. The Indian cavalry kept their swords throughout the war, apart from officers, who were given revolvers, and all ranks of the Canadian cavalry also held on to their swords. British cavalry carried carbines (a type of rifle) as well, but the sword and lance were easier to use while the horse was moving fast.

So did the cavalry ever ride across no-man's-land?

No, they did not. When everyone realized that cavalry wasn't going to be used in great charges against the enemy in the First World War, cavalry soldiers took their place with ordinary soldiers and were armed with the same weapons as the other soldiers.

What was mustard gas?

Both sides in the war were looking for new weapons that might help them win, since the trench warfare of the Western Front didn't seem to be achieving very much apart from killing large numbers of men. One of the new weapons was poisonous gas — at first the gas chlorine, which was first released in 1915. The gas injured solders' lungs, and if they were exposed to it for a long time it could kill.

Both sides used gas of different types, and as the war continued more deadly gases were used. Whoever was using the gas had to be careful: if the wind blew in the wrong direction it could end up gassing the wrong troops — this happened in

September 1915 at Loos, when gas released from cylinders was blown back towards British troops.

Mustard gas was one of the gases used by both sides. It caused victims' skin to break out in yellow blisters, could temporarily blind soldiers, and attacked the lungs.

About three in every hundred gas attack victims died, although mustard gas was more deadly than chlorine gas. But poison gas could have lasting effects, and could make solders ill for the rest of their lives. Poison gas attacks continued throughout the war because they were effective at clearing enemy positions, and each side in the war developed sophisticated gas masks — there were even gas masks for horses.

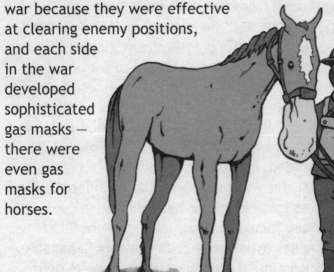

What was a Zeppelin?

A Zeppelin was a
type of German
airship, a bit like
a motorized and
steerable hot-air
balloon, but filled
with hydrogen
instead of air. They
looked like giant
floating cigars.

A crashed Zeppelin.

During the First World War, Britain came
under attack from the air for the first time when
Zeppelins attacked the east coast of England and
London in 1915, dropping explosive bombs and
fire bombs, which were designed to set buildings
blazing. Zeppelins could turn off their engines and
move silently at high altitudes to make surprise
attacks. 557 British civilian men, women and
children were killed and about 1,300 injured.
Terror spread. For the first time ever in Britain, this
was total war — civilians were being killed at home
as well as soldiers on the battlefields.

To make them airborne, airships were filled
with the gas hydrogen, which is highly flammable.
Surprisingly, firing ordinary bullets at a Zeppelin
didn't have much effect — the bullets whizzed

straight through and out the other side, and the airship kept moving. It took time to work out how to shoot down the Zeppelins, but eventually a combination of bullets, including special flaming bullets, meant that the airships could be shot down and by the end on August 1918, Zeppelin attacks on London and other cities stopped.

After the war, Zeppelins continued to be used as passenger aircraft, and made regular flights across the Atlantic. After an accident in 1937, which killed 35 people, the airships stopped being made.

Were bombs dropped from planes?

The Wright brothers made the world's first heavier-than-air powered flight in 1903, yet only eight years later Italy was flying the first ever military planes in its war against Turkey. Planes were used in the First World War too. At first, the new invention was used to help the heavy guns work out where to aim their long-range shells, by flying over enemy territory and taking photographs of the railways, trenches and weapons. This led to fights in the air, as each side tried to shoot down the enemy's spy planes. Planes also dropped bombs — in the beginning they were thrown out of the plane by hand on to enemy trenches below, and weren't very accurate. Bombs were also dropped on enemy supplies away from battle zones, putting civilians at risk. Enemy cities began to be targeted by bomber planes, as they had been by Zeppelins. Planes changed war forever: now targets and people far away from battlefields were at risk.

Was it dangerous to be a pilot?

As aeroplanes were sent to photograph enemy positions, the enemy sent planes to shoot the spy planes down. Dramatic one-to-one aerial fights took place, at first with the pilots firing pistols at one another, and later machine guns. A pilot had to use his skill to manoeuvre his plane behind the enemy's, preferably with the sun behind him to make it hard for the enemy plane to see his position, and then fire accurately — all at the same time. Not only was flying a fighter plane difficult, it was not for the faint-hearted: fighter pilots had the most dangerous jobs in the First World War, and eight out of every ten of them were killed.

What was an air ace?

Pilots who had shot down more than five enemy planes became known as air aces, and it's not hard to see why people admired them — they took huge risks every time they flew. They became First World War celebrities, with their photos constantly in the newspapers. The most famous was Germany's air ace, Manfred von Richthofen, also known as the Red Baron. He shot down around 80 fighter planes, before he was finally shot down and killed in April 1918.

Manfred von Richthofen.

Were there tanks in the First World War?

In September 1916, the first tank ever used in warfare trundled slowly up to German trenches in France during the Battle of the Somme. At a speed of 1 mph (slower than you can walk), it machine-gunned the German trench, but was later put out of action by artillery fire. The British had succeeded in their ambition to invent an armoured fighting vehicle that could withstand bullets, drive over rough ground and demolish barbed wire.

Surprisingly, since they definitely couldn't float, tanks were invented by the Royal Navy. The navy's Landships Committee referred to the secret new invention in code as 'water tanks', in case

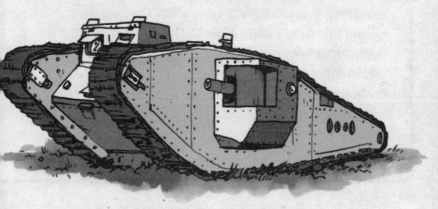

communications about them fell into enemy hands, and the name stuck. France invented tanks around the same time, and soon after the French also developed the clever rotating turret containing a gun that tanks still use today.

How many people did it take to drive a tank?

Conditions inside the first tanks were difficult, to say the least. Each tank held a crew of seven or eight men.

A Tank Crew

- The tank commander was in charge and also had to operate the steering brakes in conjunction with the driver, who had to be very skilled — passing a tank driving test wasn't easy.
- Gearsmen on either side of the tank operated gearboxes for each of the caterpillar tracks, and also manned the machine guns.
- The tank's two six-pound guns were operated by a gunner and a loader. (There were two types of tank, some with heavy machine guns instead of the six-pound guns.)

What did 'going over the top' mean?

Inside the trenches, soldiers were relatively safe from gunfire, unless they were directly hit by a shell. But every so often the soldiers climbed up over the parapet of the trench ('over the top') and advanced towards the enemy trenches. As well as on night-time raids, this happened during the big battles of the war on the Western Front.

What was it like inside the first tanks sent to war?

The crew had to carry out their complicated tasks in almost pitch darkness, because doors and hatches were shut against bullets and shrapnel — when necessary, flaps could be opened to let in light. The tanks were also very noisy and bumpy as the tank lumbered over uneven ground, and they were cramped, hot and full of fumes because of the lack of ventilation. Added to all that, the impact of a shell on the outside of the tank made the enamel paint on the inside of the tank fly off in razor-sharp splinters that whizzed around the crews' ears, and it was such a hazard that the crew wore chainmail and leather armour to protect themselves.

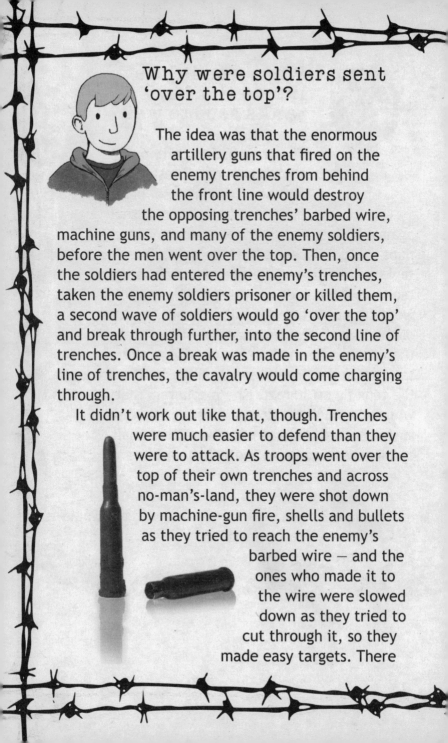

Why were soldiers sent 'over the top'?

The idea was that the enormous artillery guns that fired on the enemy trenches from behind the front line would destroy the opposing trenches' barbed wire, machine guns, and many of the enemy soldiers, before the men went over the top. Then, once the soldiers had entered the enemy's trenches, taken the enemy soldiers prisoner or killed them, a second wave of soldiers would go 'over the top' and break through further, into the second line of trenches. Once a break was made in the enemy's line of trenches, the cavalry would come charging through.

It didn't work out like that, though. Trenches were much easier to defend than they were to attack. As troops went over the top of their own trenches and across no-man's-land, they were shot down by machine-gun fire, shells and bullets as they tried to reach the enemy's barbed wire — and the ones who made it to the wire were slowed down as they tried to cut through it, so they made easy targets. There

German soldiers practising 'going over the top'.

were extremely high numbers of dead and wounded in these 'over the top' advances.

Even if a break was made in the enemy trenches, it was difficult to get weapons and other supplies forward, and successfully capture the ground. But the enemy was at an advantage: the soldiers would be within easy reach of their own supplies, and able to defend themselves.

Which was the bloodiest battle of the war?

There were several especially bloody battles during the First World War. These huge battles weren't like the Battle of Hastings, which lasted a day and had a decisive result (i.e. that the losing king was dead, and the winner was about to take his place). Some of them went on for months. The best known in Britain is the Battle of the Somme, which took place just north of the River Somme in northern France.

After a year and a half of each side shelling one another's trenches on the Western Front, with little movement either way, the battle was meant to defeat the Germans and push them back, as well as send Allied troops to help the French in a different but even worse battle at Verdun. But things didn't go well. Before the battle, the Allies bombarded the German trenches with shells, and exploded enormous underground mines, so they expected to be able to send soldiers forward and capture the German trenches fairly easily. But the big guns and mines hadn't had the effect on the enemy that the Allies had expected. On the first day of the battle, on 1 July

A British soldier tends to freshly dug war graves during the Battle of the Somme, 1916.

1916, 20,000 men died and 40,000 were wounded — that's in just one day, and those are only the British casualties. No British army in history had suffered losses like that on a single day. The Somme went on until November, and by then over a million men had been killed, wounded or captured on both sides, with 125,000 British dead, 204,000 French dead, and a staggering number of German deaths estimated between 437,000 and 680,000.

Apart from the Somme, which were the other most deadly battles?

At the same time as the Battle of the Somme, the Battle of Verdun was being fought between the French and the Germans. It began in February 1916 when the Germans attacked the fortified town of Verdun, and continued until December, by which time about a million soldiers were dead or wounded.

Soldiers walk through the remains of Chateau Wood in Ypres.

In 1917 the Third Battle of Ypres, also known as Passchendaele after the village where the battle ended, also caused terrible casualties. The area around Ypres, a town in Belgium on the Western Front, was the scene of a lot of fighting because it was a salient — the Allied front line made a bulge that stuck out into German territory. The Germans were on higher ground, so the Allied troops were at a big disadvantage. The battle was fought to advance the Allies on to higher ground, and to capture the German-controlled railway line.

Terrible downpours of summer rain, together with heavy shelling, turned the area into a mud bath — soldiers even drowned in the mud. Eventually, after months of fighting, Canadian soldiers captured Passchendaele, but the railway was still miles away. There were heavy losses on both sides: 325,000 Allied and 260,000 German dead and wounded.

What happened to prisoners of war?

Captured soldiers had to be put somewhere — you couldn't just let them loose in a forest or something — and there were literally millions of them. In just the first six months, already 1.3 million prisoners of war were held in Europe. They were put into prisons — some that already existed, and new prison camps that were built in a hurry.

What were prison camps like?

Prison camps were overcrowded, though this improved as things became more organized over the course of the war. Each side accused the other of being cruel and neglectful of its prisoners of war — the Germans were accused of not providing decent living conditions or enough food, though the lack of food was partly caused by the Allied naval blockade.

There were some escape attempts — for example, a tunnel was dug by prisoners at Holzminden Prisoner-of-War camp in 1918, and 29 officers escaped through it before the tunnel collapsed.

How many people died in the war altogether?

We will never have an accurate figure, although current estimates suggest that about 16 million people died in the First World War — about 10 million of them in the armed forces, and the rest civilian. Britain, roughly 750,000 soldiers died, most of them men aged between 19 and 34. One in every ten British men who went to fight the war didn't come back.

In other countries the death toll was worse: in Germany nearly 2 million men died (about one in six of the men who went to war); in France nearly 1.4 million soldiers died (which was also about one in every six men who went to war), and 1.7 million Russian soldiers were killed, about one in seven men. Worst hit of all was Serbia — about a fifth of all the country's men aged between 15 and 49 were killed during the war.

Deaths per number of men sent to fight

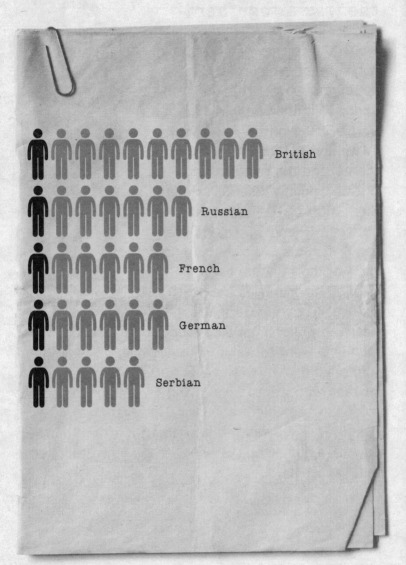

How many of them died in battle?

Most of the soldiers died in battle — around two thirds of the total — rather than from other causes, such as disease or accidents. This was in contrast to some of the wars of the previous century: in the South African War, fought between 1899 and 1902, two thirds of the deaths were due to disease. Even worse, during the Crimean War (1854—6), eight out of every ten deaths were due to disease. Some of the soldiers who died from disease in the First World War were victims of the Spanish flu that spread all around the world from 1918 — altogether, even more people died because of the Spanish flu than because of the First World War.

95

How many soldiers were wounded?

Around 21 million soldiers were wounded in the First World War. Their injuries were caused by shrapnel flying from shells fired by the big guns, bullets from rifles, pistols and machine guns, and gas (which affected soldiers' lungs, sometimes for life). The soil of the Western Front contained manure because it was fertile farmland, and unfortunately this encouraged the growth of bacteria that could make the soldiers' wounds worse, and led to amputations and even deaths.

A German soldier.

A British soldier.

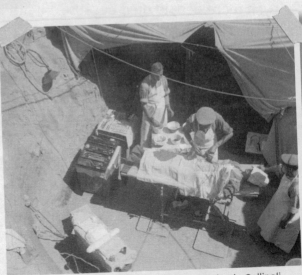

Surgery in progress at a Casualty Clearing station in Gallipoli.

What was shell shock?

Shell shock was a term first used by Dr Charles Myers, who was treating patients whose mental health was affected by the war. He called it shell shock because at first he thought his patients had brain injuries caused by shells exploding very close to them. Dr Myers changed his opinion, realizing that the soldiers were traumatized by being at war, not injured by exploding shells, but the name stuck.

Dr Charles Myers.

What do we call shell shock today?

Today we might call it 'post-traumatic stress disorder'. During the First World War, doctors recognized for the first time that war could affect soldiers mentally as well as physically, and developed ways of treating shell shock.

Where were the hospitals for the wounded?

In the British army, medical officers, helped by stretcher bearers, were responsible for taking wounded or sick soldiers from the front line to be treated nearby at a dressing station, where they'd get some basic first aid. The wounded were then taken by ambulance, either driven by a motor engine or pulled by a horse, to a Casualty Clearing Station, which was a temporary hospital staffed by doctors and nurses (this was the closest to the front line that female nurses would get).

Here, patients were treated and operated on, and then moved on to other hospitals for further treatment. Some were sent to Base Hospitals, which were larger, permanent hospitals further away from the front line in France and Belgium. Severely wounded soldiers would be sent to a hospital back in Britain on a hospital ship. Some of the hospitals specialised in particular treatments — for people who had lost limbs, or who had brain injuries, for example.

What was it like in the hospitals?

The different types of hospitals varied a lot. Near the front line, Casualty Clearing Stations were temporary tents and huts, where wounded soldiers were treated and then allocated somewhere else to go. They would either be very quiet, or madly busy when they were inundated with wounded men straight from battle, when doctors and nurses worked non-stop until they were cleared.

Did wounded soldiers ever get sent home?

Some wounded soldiers were given blood transfusions in these temporary hospitals, or kept warm in heated beds to try and revive them before they could be treated or sent to a permanent hospital somewhere else — either to a Base Hospital or back to Britain. This was known as a 'Blighty Wound'.

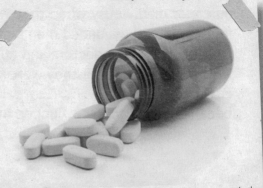

There were hospitals especially for the armed forces in Britain, but there weren't nearly enough to cope with all the casualties, so civilian hospitals were partly or completely taken over by war wounded. All these hospitals were clean and well-staffed, but they weren't quite like the hospitals we know today — they didn't have any of the electronic equipment modern hospitals rely on to monitor and treat patients, and many of the medicines used today hadn't

Antibiotics hadn't been discovered yet so the wounded were much more likely to die from infections.

been developed then. There were anaesthetics to numb patients or put them to sleep while an operation happened, but they weren't as sophisticated as the ones we have today, and carried higher risks. Maybe the most important medicines hospitals lacked in the First World War were antibiotics, which weren't discovered until more than ten years after the war. Without antibiotics, infections could kill,

The Brighton Pavilion.

so the wounded didn't have the chances of recovery they'd have in a modern hospital.

Some buildings that had a completely different purpose beforehand were converted into temporary hospitals during the war. For example, the Royal Pavilion in Brighton, an Oriental-style royal palace, became a hospital for wounded Indian troops.

What was the Home Front?

The 'fronts' of the war were where the fighting took place. At home in Britain, while there wasn't any actual fighting, people still felt the effects of the war, so it was known as the Home Front. People could be killed on the Home Front: Zeppelins and later planes bombed British towns — 1,414 were killed and 3,416 were seriously injured altogether in Zeppelin and plane attacks. Towns on the east coast, including Hartlepool, Scarborough and Yarmouth, were fired on by German ships, killing and wounding hundreds more.

What was it like in Britain and Germany while the fighting was going on?

The worst effect of the war on the Home Front was hunger, and things got worse as the war went on. German submarines targeting ships, and the

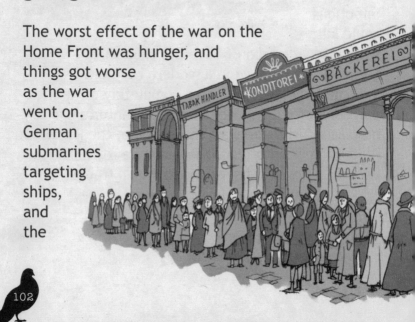

Allied naval blockade, led to food shortages in both Britain and Germany. The lack of food was made worse because the farmers who grew cereals, vegetables and fruit, and the horses that helped them, were away at the war — though women started to work on farms to help out (see page 110). Food became more expensive, and there was a lot less of it. Queues for food formed all over Europe. In Germany, the food situation was worse than in Britain, and people began to starve. Unappetizing substitute foods were suggested by the government in Germany — acorns were made into coffee and horse chestnuts into flour.

Rationing was introduced in Britain in 1918, which meant people could only have a certain amount of certain foods each week.

DEFENCE OF THE REALM.

MINISTRY OF FOOD.

BREACHES OF THE RATIONING ORDER

The undermentioned convictions have been recently obtained:—

Court	Date	Nature of Offence	Result
HENDON	29th Aug., 1918	Unlawfully obtaining and using ration books	3 Months' Imprisonment
WEST HAM	29th Aug., 1918	Being a retailer & failing to detach proper number of coupons	Fined £20
SMETHWICK	22nd July, 1918	Obtaining meat in excess quantities	Fined £50 & £5 5s. costs
OLD STREET	4th Sept., 1918	Being a retailer selling to unregistered customer	Fined £72 & £5 5s. costs
OLD STREET	4th Sept., 1918	Not detaching sufficient coupons for meat sold	Fined £25 & £2 2s. costs
CHESTER-LE-STREET	4th Sept., 1918	Being a retailer returning number of registered customers in excess of counterfoils deposited	Fined £50 & £3 3s. costs
HIGH WYCOMBE	7th Sept., 1918	Making false statement on application for and using Ration Books unlawfully	Fined £40 & £6 4s. costs

Enforcement Branch, Local Authorities Division.

If you broke the rules about rationing, you could get into a lot of trouble.

Did rationing work?

It did — people still had just about enough to eat, even though supply ships were being torpedoed by U-boats. It also made things fairer because food was more evenly shared — you couldn't buy up all the pork chops if you happened to be first in the queue.

Were there blackouts during the First World War?

Yes, towns in both Britain and Germany were under threat from enemy bombers. From October 1914, lights in many British towns weren't allowed to be shown at night, so getting around after dark could be a dim and dangerous process. These blackouts were so that towns didn't advertise where they were to enemy pilots.

What else changed at home?

The manufacture of shells, bullets and weapons for the war also had an impact on life at home, as more women now worked than ever before (see page 111). Accidents could happen: the first was a huge explosion at an explosives factory at Faversham in Kent in 1916; in 1917 there was an accident in a munitions factory at Silvertown in east London; and in 1918 a shell-filling factory in Chilwell, Nottinghamshire, exploded. The accidents killed more than 300 people and wounded hundreds more.

In Britain the government brought in new rules because of the war. The Defence of the Realm Act (known as DORA) made changes including censorship of newspapers and publishers (they were no longer allowed to say what they liked in case it wasn't favourable to the war) and imprisoning suspects without trial (in case they were enemy spies). DORA didn't allow people to hang about near tunnels or bridges (they might be planning to sabotage a road or railway), or even to whistle for a taxi (in case it was mistaken for an air-raid siren — that one does seem a bit daft).

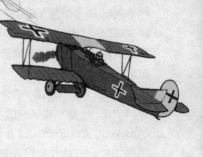

What other rules did DORA put in place?

The Defence of the Realm Act also reduced pub opening hours and the strength of alcohol because the government thought that too many people were getting drunk and their work was suffering as a result. Some of the new rules stayed in place after the war was over, including the reduced opening hours for pubs, though not the one about whistling at taxis.

What were Dead Man's Pennies?

Starting just after the war ended, the relatives of the people who'd died in the war were issued by the British government with bronze memorial discs, which became known as 'Dead Man's Pennies'. They were inscribed with the dead person's name, and the words 'He died for freedom and

A Dead Man's Penny memorial plaque.

honour' — or in some cases 'she', because around 600 women died as a result of the war. Over a million Dead Man's Pennies were issued to the closest relative of anyone killed as a result of the war in Britain or its empire. They also received a memorial scroll, and a letter from the king.

Who were 'enemy aliens'?

Anyone living in an Allied country who was originally from one of the Central Powers countries was an 'enemy alien'. People were suspicious of them — they might have their original country's best interests at heart, and could be spies. In Britain, enemy aliens were kept under close watch and thousands of them were sent to internment camps — like prisons — until after the war was over.

How did people at home find out what was happening in the war?

There were no live news feeds from the Western Front on the telly, mainly because television wouldn't be invented for another ten years. But people at home did have newspapers to read. The newspapers were regulated by the government so that they didn't influence people against the war, which might stop people from joining the armed forces, or just make everyone feel really depressed, so they tended to be quite positive about how Britain was doing in the war. People also got news of the war from letters from friends and relatives who were away fighting in it — the letters could be censored if they gave any secret information away.

Even though there was no television, there were cinemas. *The Battle of the Somme* was a silent, black-and-white film released in 1916, while the Battle of the Somme itself was still going on. Twenty million British people went to see it, some of them perpaps hoping to catch a glimpse of a friend or relative. The film showed the preparations for the battle, and some of its early stages, and presented the battle as a victory for the British. It included images of dead and wounded soldiers that made some audiences

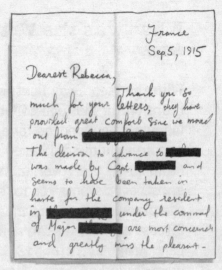

shout and scream. This was the first time a war had been filmed, and the first time people who had no experience of the Western Front could see real, up-to-date images of the war as it was being fought.

The news of the war that everyone dreaded was the news of the death of a loved one. The closest relative of a dead soldier would be notified by telegram.

What was the Women's Land Army?

With the men away fighting, there was a shortage of farm labourers to work the land and bring in the harvest. From 1915, the government encouraged women to take the place of the men, and later organized the Women's Land Army. By 1918, 113,000 women worked on the land in war service. Some of the farmers didn't like the idea

of female farm workers at all, and had to be persuaded to employ women on their farms.

As well as working on the land to produce food, women also did other jobs to replace the men who were away fighting. The highest number of women war

A woman operates a naval gun-rifling machine, 1918.

workers did jobs in munitions factories, making the enormous numbers of guns, shells and other ammunition that the army, navy and air force relied on to keep the war going. By the end of the war, there were 900,000 women working in munitions factories, and women worked in other kinds of factories too. The factories could be dangerous places to work — there were huge explosions in munitions factories during the war (see page 105) — and they could also be extremely hot: Anna Airy, one of the war artists, painted a

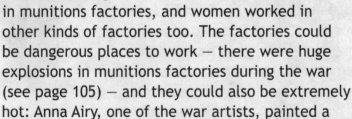

scene in a munitions factory in Hackney, London — while she was painting, the ground became so hot that the soles of her shoes were burnt off!

Added to the million women working on the land and in munitions factories, there were also 100,000 women working as nurses and 117,000 working in transport services.

Nurse Lily Cope, one of 100,000 nurses during the war.

How did the war change women's lives?

The war gave some women their first experience of work, although millions of women already worked. It wasn't respectable for middle-class married women to work before the war but lots of them found jobs as a result of it — and many of them discovered that they liked working, and especially the money and independence it gave them. The war also changed the type of work women did: some of the women who were in domestic service before the war, as servants to rich families, never went back to being servants because they found they enjoyed other work more, and were better paid and (sometimes) better treated. The war also showed women that they could work outside traditional female jobs such as dressmaking, cleaning or nursing — over half a million worked in banking, business, the civil service and transport.

When the war ended, though, lots of the jobs for women vanished. Factory jobs were given to men returning from the war in preference to women, and the huge numbers of munitions weren't needed any longer, so most of the munitions factory jobs disappeared.

Strange though it seems now, before the First World War women didn't have the right to vote in elections, and a lot of them were extremely cross about it and campaigned for women's rights before the war.

After the Armistice in 1918, most women over thirty years old in Britain were given the vote for the first time, partly to recognize how hard they'd worked during the war, but they weren't given equality with men (who could vote aged twenty-one) for another ten years.

What else did the war change for women?

Though it wasn't quite as important as the right to vote, the war also changed women's clothes: they started wearing trousers. Those long skirts could get in the way of your spade as you shovelled manure out of the pig pen or fed coal into kilns to fuel factories, so, much to the alarm of some traditional people, women did the obvious yet shocking thing and put on a pair of their husbands' or brothers' strides. After the war, women continued to

Trousers were essential work wear for fire girls and factory workers. This fire girl is practising carrying a factory worker to safety.

wear trousers for sports but rarely wore them otherwise — it took until the 1930s for trousers to find their place in women's fashion.

What did spies do in the war?

Before the war, a few German
spies were working in Britain,
attempting to gather
information about Britain's
armed forces and possible
plans for the war. But only ten
suspects were arrested in the three
years before the war began, and
there were very few British spies
working in Germany either.
Twenty-one real German
spies were arrested at
the beginning of the war,
and this fuelled people's
suspicions: everyone was on
the lookout, and thousands
of spy reports were made
to police, almost all of them unfounded — night-
time signalling to guide German airships and planes
was a popular concern. Spies were accused of
infecting horses with deadly diseases, and posing as
businessmen and circus performers.

115

How many spies were caught in Britain?

Only 31 German spies were arrested in Britain between the beginning of the war and September 1917 (there weren't any further spy trials at all after that). Nineteen of them were executed and ten imprisoned. Many of them were pretty rubbish at spying: the first to be executed, Carl Hans Lody, left lots of clues and supplied the Germans with information that was completely untrue.

The most famous spy of the war, and one of the most famous spies ever, was Mata Hari. She was a beautiful Dutch dancer who spied for the Germans against the French, and was executed in Paris in 1917.

Mata Hari.

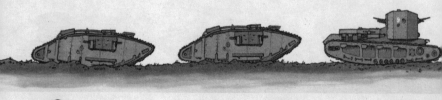

Who won the war?

After more than four years' fighting, the Allies won the war. By 1918, the German, French and British armies were all finding a shortage of men to fight. In Germany, people were starving, and the German soldiers were often hungry too. All of the armies were exhausted.

With the United States about to enter the war, Germany decided to put all its remaining energy into a last-ditch effort to win. In the spring of 1918 the Germans launched huge attacks against the Allies. For a while it looked as though the Central Powers might win — the Germans advanced further than they had since the beginning of the war. But the Allies fought back, using tanks and aircraft as well as guns, and the German army was eventually forced back.

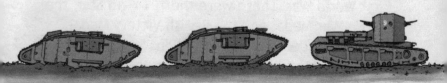

What happened next?

The defeated Germans agreed an armistice (an agreement to stop fighting). The terms of the Armistice made it impossible for Germany to carry on with the war, and Kaiser Wilhelm II gave up his crown. From 11 o'clock in the morning of 11 November 1918, the war in Western Europe was over, though it continued in other parts of the world while peace deals were worked out, and these weren't finalized until 1919.

Kaiser Wilhelm II.

What happened when the soldiers came home?

Returning British soldiers received medals: there were three different campaign medals, which were awarded to everyone who'd served in the First World War. These were the 1914–15 Star, the British War Medal and the British Victory Medal. The medals became known as 'Pip, Squeak and Wilfred' after a popular cartoon in the *Daily Mirror* which featured a dog, a penguin and a rabbit.

There were also 300,000 medals awarded for bravery during the course of the war.

Some Allied soldiers had celebrated wildly when the war ended, and once they were home they continued to have riotous parties on the anniversary of the Armistice. But because so many people had died in the war, and there were so many grieving families, the anniversary became much more solemn.

Many of the soldiers who returned from the war came back wounded — in France, this was nearly half of the men who'd fought in the war. In Britain, more than a million wounded men came home. Some of them recovered from their injuries completely, but others died, and until the early 1920s, the men who died of their wounds received full military funerals.

ounded soldiers outside the examination schools, Oxford.

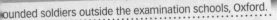

What was life like for soldiers after the war?

For the men who'd lost limbs, were blinded or who struggled to breathe because of poisoned gas, life would never be the same again. The government set up pensions for disabled ex-soldiers, though it was often barely enough to live on. Treatment was also provided, including artificial limbs (civilians weren't given free medical treatment in those days because

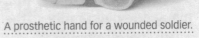

A prosthetic hand for a wounded soldier.

there was no National Health Service). Until 1922 there was a government training programme for wounded soldiers, and there were also charities that helped wounded ex-soldiers to find work.

The soldiers who were fit and well came home and took up their old jobs. Many of them found it hard to adjust to their old lives. Some men had got so used to the roar of gunfire that they couldn't sleep without it. But not everyone had jobs to go to . . .

British Prime Minister Lloyd George promised a 'land fit for heroes', but an economic slump, because of the massive cost of the war, and high unemployment in the 1920s meant that many ex-soldiers ended up poor and miserable. The first poppy appeal was held in 1921 to raise money for ex-servicemen who needed it — poppies were chosen as a symbol because they thrived in the churned-up ground of the battlefields in Belgium and France.

After the Armistice in 1918, one of the changes made by the British government was to extend the vote to all men aged over 21, at the same time as giving women the right to vote for the first time. Before that, four out of every ten men over the age of 21 didn't have the right to vote in elections, because to qualify for the vote men had to own a certain amount of property. It's surprising now to think that many of the men who were fighting in the First World War didn't have a say in the government of their country.

How did the war change the world?

The First World War was the first war to be waged on land, sea and in the air, and because of it empires collapsed, new countries were created, and the way was paved for future wars. In 1919 there was a conference in Paris to discuss what should happen now that the war was finished. These are some of the huge changes that happened because of the war:

- Imperial Germany was one of the four empires that ended with the First World War (the others were Austria-Hungary, Russia and the Ottoman Empire). In Europe, this meant that borders were redrawn, new countries created and old ones re-established, including Poland, Hungary, Austria, Czechoslovakia (now the Czech Republic and Slovakia) and Yugoslavia (now Croatia, Serbia, Kosovo and others). New problems were created along with some of the countries.
- Germany was allowed to keep only a small army and navy, and had to pay compensation to the Allies for starting the war. There was a lot of hardship in Germany because of its dire financial situation. However, they did not pay a single penny to France and Belgium despite the terms of the Treaty of Versailles and started to rebuild their armed forces.

- France wanted there to be far harsher terms settled on Germany at the end of the war as it had been invaded by them twice within living memory. It called for an army of occupation to be moved into Germany. None of the other victorious allies had the men or the desire to occupy Germany. The French believed that they had been let down by Britain and America and it was only a matter of time before Germany attacked again.

- Russia gave away huge chunks of its empire when it left the war after its revolution. In the civil war that followed, even more Russian people died than had been killed in the First World War.

- The Ottoman Empire split up. Some of its territories, including modern-day Iraq, were divided among the winning nations. One of the Turkish commanders in the battle for Gallipoli, Mustafa Kemal, founded the modern country of Turkey in the 1920s.

- The Central Powers' colonies in Africa, Asia and the Pacific were given to the empires of winning nations.

- Although the British Empire got bigger after the war with new territories from the Central Powers, some countries within the empire — including Canada, Australia, New Zealand and India — decided they wanted to be more independent.

- One and a half million Indian soldiers volunteered to fight in the war and made a big contribution to the Allied victory. After the war, India was promised more independence from Britain, but the promise seemed empty and anti-British feeling began to grow. Things were made a lot worse when British troops fired on an Indian

political demonstration at Amritsar in 1919, killing 379 people and injuring about 1,200 more. It took a long time for the British to leave India, but the First World War started the process.

- There were social changes too: in Britain the voting system was made fairer (see page 121), and the class structure — with aristocrats running things and ordinary working people doing as they were told — became less rigid. The government began to take more of a role in housing and looking after the people who'd suffered for their country during the war.

The peace lasted until 1939, when Adolf Hitler, who had fought in the First World War, led Germany into the Second World War.

Hitler giving a speech at Nuremberg.

Why do we remember it now?

In 2009 the last surviving soldier died, aged 111. But we still remember the war because it was an important turning point in history, and because so many people died — 16 million people from all around the world. If you look back into your family history, you might find that you're connected to the First World War, maybe through a relative who fought in it.

In the UK on Remembrance Sunday — the closest Sunday to 11 November, when the Armistice was signed in 1918 — people remember the First World War with a two-minute silence at 11 a.m. The

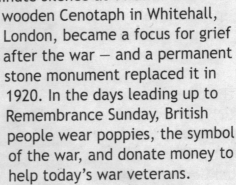

wooden Cenotaph in Whitehall, London, became a focus for grief after the war — and a permanent stone monument replaced it in 1920. In the days leading up to Remembrance Sunday, British people wear poppies, the symbol of the war, and donate money to help today's war veterans.

Each country remembers the war — and their dead, in a different way.

What effects of the war can I see every day?

The countryside of Belgium and France is covered with the effects of the First World War: vast cemeteries for the soldiers who died on the battlefields of the Western Front, and massive craters left when underground mines exploded. But there are reminders closer to home too: there's almost certainly a war memorial somewhere near where you live, engraved with the names of the people who died in the First World War who came from the area. These memorials were designed and paid for by local communities in the 1920s, so they're all different from one another. There are around 100,000 war memorials in the United Kingdom, commemorating the First World War and other wars.

How do I find out more?

You could start by finding out about the First World War in your local area — how many soldiers went to fight, whether there were any army training camps nearby, or hospitals for the wounded, or munitions factories. There might be a museum where you live that has this kind of information.

The Imperial War Museum was set up in 1917 as a record of the First World War, and today it can give you a unique insight into what it was like to be involved in the war. If you can't make a trip to IWM London, or to Manchester to visit IWM North, or to one of IWM's other branches, you could have a look at the museum's website.

The Imperial War Museum, London.

Other museums:

The National Army Museum, London
The National Museum of the Royal Navy, Portsmouth
The Royal Air Force Museum, London, and Cosford,
   Shropshire
The Tank Museum, Bovington, Dorset

Websites:

www.iwm.org.uk
www.nationalarchives.gov.uk
www.cwgc.org

Books:

*The Trenches: A First World War Soldier,
   1914–1918 (My Story)* by Jim Eldridge
   (Scholastic, 2008)

*Road to War: A First World War Girl's Diary,
   1917 (My Story)* by Valerie Wilding
   (Scholastic, 2008)

Glossary

Air aces Fighter pilots who shot down more than five enemy planes became known as air aces and some became First World War celebrities

Allies The name used to refer to the side comprised of Russia, France and the British Empire during the First World War

Armistice An agreement to stop fighting

Battle of the Somme One of the most deadly battles of the First World War on the Western Front

Casualty Clearing Stations Temporary hospitals staffed by doctors and nurses for wounded soldiers

Cenotaph A stone monument to the dead of the First World War in Whitehall, London. The scene of the annual commemoration ceremony in Britain on Remembrance Sunday

Central Powers The name used to refer to the German, Austro-Hungarian, Ottoman and Bulgarian side during the First World War

Conscientious Objectors Men who refused to fight in the war, either because they thought all wars were wrong or they didn't think this particular war was right

Dead Man's Penny Bronze memorial plaque issued to the relatives of British and British Empire soldiers who had died in the war

Defence of the Realm Act A set of new rules brought in by the British government because of the war

Going over the top The term used to describe soldiers climbing over the top of the trenches and advancing on foot towards the enemy

Home Front The 'fronts' of the war were where the fighting took place. At home in Britain the effects of the war were still felt so this became known as the Home Front

Imperial War Museum A museum set up in 1917 to record the experiences of the people of Britain and the British Empire during the First World War

Kaiser The German Emperor and war leader

Messenger dogs Dogs used by the army that were trained to carry messages on the battlefields in metal tubes attached to their collars

Messenger pigeons Homing pigeons used to carry

messages clipped to their legs in metal containers

Mustard gas A poisonous gas used as a weapon in the war

No-man's-land The strip of ground separating two lines of trenches

Order of the White Feather Founded at the beginning of the war in order to shame young men into joining the army

'Pals' Battalions Groups of friends or colleagues who fought together in the same fighting unit

Prison camps Hurriedly built camps to contain prisoners of war (captured enemy soldiers)

Rationing Food shortages during the war meant that rationing was introduced, so people could only have a certain amount of food each week

Remembrance Sunday The closest Sunday to 11 November when the Armistice was signed in 1918, to remember those who died in war

Semaphore A coded system used by soldiers sending messages with flags

Shell shock A term used to describe the condition

suffered by those who were mentally affected by war. Today it is called post-traumatic stress disorder

Trenches A complex system of deep ditches that were dug to protect soldiers from artillery and gun fire

War artists Artists sponsored by the government to paint eyewitness scenes of the war

War poets People involved in the war who wrote poems about it. They were not sponsored by the government

Western Front The battle zone running from the Belgian coast in the north, through Belgium and France down to the Alps at the border with Switzerland

Women's Army Auxiliary Corps An organization of women involved in supporting the army

Women's Land Army An organization made up of women who worked on the land while men were away fighting

Zeppelin A type of German airship filled with hydrogen instead of air. Zeppelins attacked the east coast of England and London during the war, dropping explosives and fire bombs

Alphabetical index of main topics

Acknowledgements

With grateful thanks to Abigail Ratcliffe, Grant Rogers, Terry Charman and all those at IWM for their historical expertise, encouragement and support in making this book a reality.

Picture credits

JO FOSTER

WHY Would a DOG NEED A PARACHUTE?

Why did the Second World War start?

Could you still buy sweets?

Why were spies important?

Find out the answers to these and lots of other exciting questions in this brilliantly informative book which will tell you everything you ever needed to know about the Second World War.